In Search of Balance

THE BUSINESS OWNERS GUIDE TO
BUILDING A BUSINESS AND A LIFE

Kevin Minton

ChiefExecutiveBoards.com

Kevin Minton
kevin@chiefexecutiveboards.com

Ordering Information:
Quantity sales. Special discounts are available on quantity purchases by corporations, associations, and others. For details, contact the "Special Sales Department" at the address above.

In Search of Balance/ Kevin Minton. —1st ed.
ISBN 978-0-9904941-3-3

Tim Gase, President of Peerless Saw Company

"You're not going to find a better group or organization where you can share your problems with people who are having the exact same problems you're dealing with."

Prior to joining Chief Executive Boards in 1996, Tim Gase was a recently installed company president looking for guidance.

"I was president of Peerless Saw. I'd been there since '95. I needed a peer group of some kind to piggyback on to help me. It was the biggest jump in position I had ever had. CE-BI was a good steppingstone to find a peer group I could work with, who could give me some help on questions that nobody else could.

"Probably the best thing about Chief Executive Boards was during the time I was the president, not the owner, of Peerless Saw, and within four years I had the opportunity to buy the business. If it hadn't been for the support of the group and my advisors... I don't know if it would have ever happened."

"There was one gentleman in the group who had bought and sold a number of companies, and he gave me a lot of great advice. When he was helping us try to buy the business, his best advice to me at that time was 'don't go cheap on your attorneys or accountants. You hire the best to help you get the job done. It'll pay its weight in gold.' We followed both of his recommendations and they shaped the outcome into what it was."

"Joining CEBI – it really changed me. I tell people if I can walk away from one of our meetings with one new, good idea, it's worth every minute spent.

"You're not going to find a better group or organization where you can share your problems with people who are having the exact same problems you're dealing with. You can't go home and talk to your wife about them, or family, or friends, because they don't understand what you're going through as an owner. Every one of these individuals can offer advice on how to deal with these problems."

Rich Haggins, CEO of US&S

"I don't work as hard as I used to. I learned to delegate more. I learned the business isn't about Rich Haggins."

"I've been a member of Chief Executive Boards a little over four years. When I first joined Chief Executive Boards, I had a partner. Part of what we were doing was trying to figure out his exit strategy, and the strategy for me to take over the company.

"Once I joined Chief Executive Boards, I picked up a lot of techniques on how to move forward and how to work with my partner. I was able to structure a buy out, and now I'm the sole owner of the company. And, I think that was largely due to my involvement in Chief Executive Boards."

"When you think about the benefits of Chief Executive Boards, there are many. One word to describe it might be 'holistic.' The group helps you think about things— not just financially, but also from a perspective of thinking about the people part of the business. How to treat people. How to get people focused on one direction."

"One of things in my business in particular is a succession plan for my daughter. Right now, my daughter is vice president of business development and we're looking at her coming in and taking over as president of the company one day."

"One great benefit of being involved in my Chief Executive Board is the exposure to new ideas. Through the group I was introduced to the book *Every Family's Business*. I would have never known about that if it wasn't for being involved in the board. I read that book. Had my daughter read the book. We're lock-step in moving along this road of succession planning in our family business."

"Chief Executive Boards is going to expose you to so many things that, when you're trying to run a business, grow a business, you just don't have the opportunity to have a dedicated board help you vet real hard situations.

"You know what's interesting is that the things that you learn is that...you think you're by yourself, on your own in this journey, but you're not. When you have a problem that you need to handle on your own, you have a whole group backing you. And, when you have a solid board behind you, who you can talk to confidentially, you get so much more done.

"I don't work as hard as I used to because I learned to delegate more, I learned the business isn't about Rich Haggins— the business is the business. And, when I talk to my team, the most important element other than them is the company staying in business."

Contents

Introduction

It's lonely at the top.

As a business owner and CEO, you don't have anyone to talk to who understands what you're going through as you run your company (and its impact on your personal life)— let alone someone who can offer helpful, actionable advice and counsel.

Your spouse is tired of hearing about it. Your friends and neighbors just don't get it. And you can't always confide in your business partners or seek input from managers or executives.

You don't have the people you need to bounce ideas off of, discuss challenges, keep you accountable when necessary, tell you if you're on-track or off-track, or simply share what's bothering you.

The backdrop to all of this is that the world is more complex than it's ever been and running a business has never been more challenging. You're faced with rapid and unpredictable change that you, as a business owner, have to navigate on a regular basis... often without enough support.

At the same time, you're trying to build a business that grows your personal wealth while serving your customers to the best of your ability. You're trying to put together a team around you to free up your time and create that freedom you crave. After all, it's why you got into business.

And yet, all these goals seem far out of reach.

In this book, you're going to discover how the most successful business owners in the world navigate chaotic and challenging times by surrounding themselves with a group of seasoned peer advisors, and by using a structure for getting the most value from their *Chief Executive Board.*

Inside this book you'll discover:

- How to leverage a Chief Executive Board to helps you make sense of changes in the marketplace.

- How to elicit meaningful, needle moving ideas from your Board.

- How to improve your decisions using the "wisdom of the Board" to ensure that you're making the right choice.

For the entrepreneurs who follow the plan you're about to read, it's the secret to making better decisions, creating more balance in your life, having better cash flow, and a more valuable business.

If you've been going it alone, you're at the mercy of the chaotic world. You'll often second guess your decisions and, you will not have access to the most up-to-date best practices.

You'll continue to work in your business... and rarely (or never) on it. Which means, you don't own a business, you own a job.

You won't enjoy the benefits of close fellowship and camaraderie with the only people who really understand what you're going through. You'll miss out on practical help from other people who are building businesses and aspiring to achieve the same goals as you.

You'll continue to struggle to balance your business, home life, and personal relationships. Experience unending stress and worry. And it'll only get worse as time passes.

CHAPTER 1

It's Lonely at the Top

Your #1 goal is to create business value. You want to enjoy personal wealth and a comfortable lifestyle for your family. And, you want to build a company that grows beyond you, that you can sell at retirement or when you're ready for a new venture.

But, right now, you're not on that road. You don't have the processes and systems in place. The business is you— which means you don't have the freedom you desire.

Are you scared of what would happen if you didn't go into the office for a few days? If you don't feel like it could survive without you– that's not a good sign.

As a business owner, you have no one to turn to who understands the challenges you face on a daily basis as you run your business, not to mention the stress that comes with it.

You lay awake at night, doing "math on the ceiling," contemplating where your next clients are coming from, how you'll make payroll next month, and countless other issues that can create chaos in your business.

It feels like everything rests on your shoulders. And, if your business is structured so that everything is tied to your direct involvement, your success or failure likely depend on you (and only you).

You have a lot at stake. Your investment in your business, whether you bought it or built it from the ground up, could be tied to a personal guarantee. If the business fails, will you lose your savings... your house?

That's a lot of pressure.

Who Can You Turn To?

As you face major business challenges, you feel like you have to bear that pressure by yourself. You often can't talk about your concerns, struggles, significant people issues, or big strategic decisions with your team.

Your spouse might be supportive but not understand the challenges you face or know how to help, or you don't want to burden them with worry. Either way, it's a strain on the relationship.

Your friends and neighbors, while they might be willing to listen, probably don't understand what you're going through either or know how to help.

You might have put up a false front as you go through all this–to your employees, your family and friends, and fellow business owners you meet in the community or at events. You have a smile on your face, while suffering inner turmoil.

You don't have anyone you can trust with the truth.

Because you have no one "qualified" to talk to and bounce ideas off of, it's harder to make effective decisions. Sometimes you have trouble making a decision at all. Often business owners just freeze because they're not sure what to do.

That has its own set of consequences because, in this environment, it's difficult to adjust and adapt to changes in the market in a timely manner.

You Don't Have to Do Things the "Hard Way"

It's lonely at the top. And if you don't recognize it, it could be because you want to believe everything is fine.

Or perhaps you know it isn't but are steaming ahead anyway because you don't see an alternative. Or you simply find it hard to ask for help, or think nobody could possibly understand what you're going through.

Without any feedback or outside perspective on the correct way forward, you realize you've made some bad decisions.

You do not have to learn things the hard way every time. If you're stuck, you do not have to figure things out on your own.

It *is* lonely at the top... and there *is* something you can do about it, especially if you're facing a tough decision and have been stuck for a while, unsure of what to do next.

Not only that, but you'll see your relationships with employees and business partners improve, not to mention those relations with your family. Your lifestyle and quality of life improve, while the time you spend working in the business – especially on the things you don't enjoy – decreases.

Along the way, you gain confidence and tangible results that lead to your company becoming a cash engine. And you also see a boost in the intrinsic value of your company. These are the intangibles that many business owners are too busy to pay enough attention to.

Essentially, you need help spotting issues that could be harming your company. So, while you might realize you need to improve your product, for example, you do not recognize other gaps in your business that diminish its value.

CHAPTER 2

Creating Your Cash Engine

Why did you really go into business for yourself? There can be many motivations.

But at the basic level, you seek to build personal wealth. That's why you took the risk.

You might want to leave a legacy for your family, a valuable asset that you nourish and protect, so that it can be passed down for generations.

Or perhaps, you're working towards a big cash event and pay-day when you sell the business down the road. You want it to have enough value to attract buyers and investors.

Along the way, you want to make employees and customers happy.

No matter what, you want to enjoy the financial benefits of being a business owner *right now*. That's why you don't work for somebody else.

But... your overarching goal of growing business value and building a cash engine is out of reach. Trying to fly solo– where everything depends on you and you have no place to vet ideas– means you haven't been able to execute ideas as quickly as you should.

You feel like you're playing catch up all the time... frequently missing big opportunities.

As a result it's been difficult to build the sort of business you need to create the wealth you want, both today, in terms of your current cash engine, and in terms of the future.

To reach these goals, you need to turn your business into a real cash engine that consistently grows in value. This will give you the lifestyle you want now, and set you up for a transition somewhere down the road.

When that transition takes place, whether it's passing on to your kids, selling, or liquidating, is not always up to you. Sometimes you pick the timing, sometimes it's the other way around. And, it could be much sooner than you think.

That's why it's important to start making changes now.

Barriers to a Healthy, Growing Business

Unfortunately, many businesses are not structured or run in a way that helps owners reach that goal efficiently without having to put in 90 or 100 hours a week– and even then, they're not reaching their full potential.

Many owners are great at what they do, but not at reading the financial reports of the business, which can lead to stumbling blocks.

For example, many think that all growth is good. But uncontrolled growth can put a company out of business very quickly. We've seen people run their business into the ground because they grew too fast and ran out of capital to fund the type of growth trajectory they had created.

You don't have all the answers. You don't *need* to have all the answers. But, you do need a place to go, and a group you can turn to, for those answers.

You don't have to reinvent the wheel every time a business challenge comes along. You don't have to make the same mistakes others have already made– and solved.

The goal is a more profitable and valuable business – and it's possible, with the ideas I'll share in the rest of this book to double your Compound Annual Growth Rate (CAGR), while you create even more peace of mind, more personal freedom, and more time for things you want to do.

You won't just have a more successful business but also have a group of people encouraging you to work towards a better balance in your life, including better health and wellness– which can make you more productive.

CHAPTER 3

Better Health, Peace of Mind, and Life Balance

Your health is suffering. Your relationships are suffering. You're stressed all the time, and it's taking its toll.

This whole situation is killing your life outside of work because you're constantly stressed about the business. You feel very alone.

For many business owners, the concept of work/life balance is a cruel joke. Studies show that 80% of successful people are what we call "grinders." The key to their success is grinding their way through it, working early mornings, late nights, many weekends and growing their business through sheer will and hard work.

But, there is not much balance with the other aspects of your life when you're grinding: your relationships with your kids and your spouse, your spiritual life, and more. Plus, you're not building a sustainable business if it means everything is on your shoulders and requires you working 60, 80, or 100 hours a week.

You can't sell a business like that. And in the present day, you can't really enjoy the fruits of your labor. You're not free to do so because you're tied to the business.

You have to get out of this mode. It's impacting your life, your family, and your health. Your business is suffering too– what's going on with you personally always impacts your work.

These are not lightweight issues, so don't treat them as an afterthought.

This can take a severe toll on your physical health and wellness, the balance between work and your time at home, and your mental health and peace of mind. Constant stress. Tension. Conflict. Resentment. It's all swirling around you every day, often compromising your ability to plan and execute strategic decisions.

Family problems caused by extreme work habits and the stress that comes from dealing with major business decisions or strategic moves are made worse when you get called away from the business to deal with them. That leads to more problems in the company in your absence.

Similarly, health issues caused by the stress and anxiety of running your business will only make you less effective at running your business, thereby causing more worry... it's a doom loop.

The Benefits of Business "Self-Care"

What many people don't realize is that you must take care of yourself first, otherwise you're of no use to anybody else.

When you have that, not only will your business and personal financial health be on target, but you'll feel better, experience better personal relationships, and have real peace of mind.

You won't be wondering where the next client is coming in or whether you're going to make payroll–you'll be able to sleep well at night instead of doing math on the ceiling at two in the morning.

When your family, business, and spiritual lives thrive, along with physical health and positive mindset, you can experience true peace of mind knowing that you're headed in the right direction.

What's the solution?

Yes, you need systems to run the day-to-day of your business. You must delegate tasks so you can focus on strategic thinking – not putting out fires. For that, you need a capable and dependable team.

But it's easier said than done to delegate, find effective employees, and put systems in place so the business can run without your day-to-day involvement. This is especially true when you built the business from the ground up.

When you can't put these elements in place it has a big impact on your family and spouse. It's the reason that drives many business owners into divorce.

They have all this stress. They have so much riding on their shoulders. They have this worry about money. But they don't really communicate well with anyone about it.

The problem gets worse and worse. It builds resentment in your personal relationships. It can ruin friendships outside of business, but it is especially impactful on marriages.

Your Chief Executive Board can be instrumental in helping you find the right direction– and make the right decisions to put you on the right road.

CHAPTER 4

Focus on Your Strengths... and Avoid the Work You Don't Like to Do

As far as the current success of your business, what got you here won't help you at the next level... or get you to the next stage of growth.

What you had to do when you started your business is probably not what you need to be doing when it becomes a million-dollar business or a $5 million, $10 million, or $20 million business... or even a $100 million business.

You are still very capable, but the company and your role in it changes as it evolves.

That was your goal when you started the business anyway, right? You weren't planning to be "in the trenches" every day on the frontline. You envisioned taking a step back to focus on the big picture, leaving the day-to-day to your team. A true business leader that provides guidance, but lets the team figure out the details.

When your business hits a certain level, you should be able to step back. Not just in reducing your workload, but in ensuring that workload is focused on planning and strategic direction... and tasks you enjoy doing (and that you're good at).

Everybody has their core competencies. When you focus on yours, and let others take over what they're good at, everything runs more smoothly. The change in your business' growth can be dramatic.

But many business owners don't know how to get out of their own way–and out of the way of their team. They don't know what they should focus on in order to bring the most value to the company and generate more money.

Often it means outsourcing or hiring for aspects of the business you're not good at or don't enjoy–playing to your strengths. We've come across many business leaders who are good idea people—for them, hiring a person to focus on execution and implementation is a natural progression.

This is probably the number one thing that holds a business back: the owner. Relinquishing control of certain aspects of your business is one of the hardest things many business owners have to do.

If they don't, it not only holds them and the company back, but it diminishes value and stalls growth– maybe even causes a contraction.

Get Out of Your Own Way

The top skillset needed to grow a small business into a medium-sized business is delegation: taking things off your plate that you shouldn't be doing. That, and emotional intelligence. If those two elements are missing, it impacts the company's growth.

When you have a smoothly running business, you do not have to do the work you don't want to do because you have an effective internal team.

You must free up your time so you're working on things you're the best at, and you have taken everything else off your plate. And, you have a team around you that can make that happen by taking on those other tasks... and not delegating it back to you.

This is not a "one and done" process. It takes time and effort. But it's key if you want to grow the business beyond yourself. Otherwise you've just given yourself a job, with the added stress of being the boss, too.

Life and circumstances are always changing. New opportunities appear. Challenges pop up. What worked yesterday might not work the next.

You must be adaptable. You must find new solutions to fix new problems.

You must be prepared to deal with things that come at you from left field, or new obstacles and challenges. When you're not doing every little thing in your business, you have the ability– and assistance– to deal with new situations head on as they come at you.

CHAPTER 5

Work on the Business, Not in the Business

When you started your company, you were intimately involved in every aspect of the business. The truth is that back then, without you, your vision, and your dedication, the business probably would have failed.

You might still have the attitude that the business can't operate without you. But at a certain level, growth stalls if the business is all about you.

You might understand that on some level. However, you're stuck– consciously or unconsciously. You don't know how to get yourself out of this mode.

In many cases, business owners are controlled by their calendar and schedule, pulled into situations they should not be as opposed to the high-value initiatives you should be focused on.

It's like you have a jar. You put five or six rocks in it—those are your most high-value initiatives you want to work on for your business. After that, there's room for pebbles and sand. But, if you start with filler, your jar won't have room for major projects.

What about those small things? They get picked up by employees or outsourced.

Your focus must remain more strategic. You need a mindset that helps you avoid getting bogged down in the day-to-day as your growing business has more employees and assets... and complexity.

Everybody wants to be working on their business instead of in it. But, they don't know how to get there.

Instead of being hands-on, involved in every project as you did in the early days, making every decision, you must focus on the strategic moves that will take the business to the next level.

The reality is that the time you spend working on something that could feasibly be delegated is a missed opportunity, time you could have spent on planning, coming up with a strategic direction, and building your business as a result.

It's hard to make the transition. You might feel like it'll all fall apart if you're not directly involved in most or all aspects of your business. You might feel like nobody else gets it.

Your Chief Executive Board can help you get to that point of being more hands-off.

First, some ground rules for delegating to your team:

1. Determine which tasks you currently handle that could be handed off. One place to start: tasks you don't enjoy or are not good at.

2. Figure out who is the right person on your team for the job. Not everybody is suited to taking on such responsibility.

3. Explain to this person why you're delegating this task and why you chose them.

4. Provide a clear explanation on how to do the job– and give the proper training and resources to do it right.

5. Ensure the team member understands what success looks like.

6. Check their progress and results– give feedback as needed. You can't expect people to improve if you don't tell them what they're doing right and wrong in a constructive way.

There is room for guidance and questions in the early days. And there can be some intensive work when you first hand-off a task. But, take care that employees don't delegate their task right back to you and get you just as involved in the task as you were before. You don't want to become the bottleneck again.

A key point to make here is that aside from the actual work, you must also delegate responsibility for getting the task done. And give the employee the authority they need to do so.

This could mean using a strategy or method you wouldn't have. But giving employees room to be innovative can lead to impactful new solutions. That is sometimes the magic of delegation.

Most importantly, delegation frees you up to do the work you must to grow your business and take it to the next level.

CHAPTER 6

The People Who Will Help Transform Your Business

Your business is not growing as fast as it should. You know you need more focus on necessary strategic planning. You're working too many hours for too few positive results. You hesitate to pull the trigger on important decisions.

As a result, you're stressed and worried. You're working all the time, which isn't why you got into business for yourself. And it's all taking its toll on your personal life.

But it can all change.

You can start to work on your business, instead of in it, to determine the right strategic direction for your business and creating and executing a plan to get there.

You can focus on your strengths and stick with tasks your good at – and enjoy.

You can grow your business into a cash engine that is sustainable long term and is well on its way for a profitable sale down the road.

By focusing on working on the business and focusing on strengths, the business is no longer all consuming. That's how you grow business value and improve stress, relationships, and all the rest. No more 80-hour weeks. No more drama at home.

As we've stated, you can't get this type of support from friends, family, or a spouse. Your team probably won't give you the help and feedback you need, whether they are not comfortable or unable to do so.

Continuing to go it alone and shoulder the whole burden yourself is not an option. You can't achieve the results you need simply put; you lack the expertise and experience... your constant second-guessing slows you down... and there's just not enough time in a day.

The way you achieve this is by plugging into a group of likeminded, success-oriented business owners in a *confidential* environment where you can discuss issues related to your business, such as employees, business partners, finances, operations, marketing, business development, and anything else related to your business.

That's where your Chief Executive Board, comes in. This is not a casual gathering over coffee, an infrequently scheduled meeting where nothing much gets accomplished, or an ineffective networking event.

This is a formal meeting, regularly scheduled, with a strict agenda. Everybody in attendance is focused on making the most of the time to help solve problems, keep you focused in the right direction, and clear hurdles prohibiting you from achieving success.

The right type of CEO peer group will give you access to:

- Best business practices from business owners who've gone through what you did and came out the other side stronger. You can shorten your learning curve by taking advantage of their experiences (good and bad) and expertise.

- An impartial sounding board that will tell you like it is. Those on your team might not feel comfortable being honest with you about how they feel about your decisions. But fellow business owners, without a stake in your business, will be honest.

- Accountability, so that not only do you say you're focusing your strengths, executing plans, and other tasks that will move the needle, but you're actually doing it. It's important to note that you'll be accountable for *making* decisions you say you need to make. The group won't tell you what to do– although they'll have suggestions and insights. But, they expect you to make the decision, whichever way you choose.

- Support when it comes to issues outside of the business like the impact on your family and personal life. They've all been there— and they'll share the benefit of their experience.

Your Own Board of Advisors

The CEO peer group can help you see gaps– or even growth opportunities– in your company and improve your business's intrinsic value. That outside perspective can be invaluable. Often, you're too close to really see what's going on with your business. Emotion can make you blind to pitfalls and potential solutions.

As a member of a CEO peer group, you'll get help taking advantage of opportunities for growth, input on potential new strategies, and assistance in making tough decisions

What you discuss in your peer group is completely confidential– word of what was talked about in your board meeting does not leave the room. This makes this peer group your ideal sounding board and place get professional and personal support and feedback.

You can be open and vulnerable. In fact, your peer group may be the only place you feel comfortable really opening up, getting real, and dealing with the challenges and opportunities in front of you.

You can discuss your personal life challenges as well. Because at this point, it's all intertwined, isn't it? And, many business owners need help blending work and life at home and staying healthy, physically and mentally.

The topics discussed are up to the members of the board– it's completely self-driven. That means timely advice when you need it— pressing issues become priority.

You're Not Alone Anymore

Many business owners can feel indecisive on larger issues; they hesitate to pull the trigger on significant decisions because they only have themselves to debate the pros and cons with. Your peer group can help you go over the pros and cons– including some you may not realize. The decision is ultimately yours, but you don't have to solve these problems yourself.

From your peer group, you can expect validation if you're going in the right direction or advice to steer a bit differently if you're off-track.

Over the long-term, participation in a CEO peer group not only helps you make better business decisions, but your overall business knowledge and acumen starts to increase thanks to the topics that are being brought up in the group.

You learn from the feedback you receive directly from your fellow members but also the advice they give to others.

Going at it alone can be dangerous. With your board, your CEO peer group, you'll become part of a collective of elite business owners, presidents, and CEOs who help each other get better results... and can help each other watch out for blind spots.

It's unlike any business relationship you have outside of working with mentor or business coach.

CHAPTER 7

Your Impartial Sounding Board

How would having a board of advisors, a smart group of individuals likely possessing more than 200 years of collective experience as business owners, change the trajectory of your company?

Virtually every decision you need to make has been made, you just need to plug into the right group of peers. That's wisdom and experience– knowledge-based capital– that you can surround yourself with at Chief Executive Boards.

The idea of the CEO peer group is to create a brain trust of individual business owners who do not have a financial stake in your business and don't work for you. An impartial outside observer can tell you like it is, be brutally honest, yet supportive.

They won't be the "yes-men" who may be surrounding you right now. It doesn't matter how smart or qualified your people are. Think about it... is an executive on your management team going to tell you your ideas won't work?

And if you're missing the mark, you'll be challenged and asked the tough questions: is this the real issue you should be working on? Are you clearing the obstacles out of the way you must to move in a positive direction?

With your CEO peer group, you have a built-in group of "outsiders" who might see solutions and opportunities you have missed, a team you can trust to get in a huddle with you when you need a game-winning play... or just need to move the ball down the field.

A peer group member can be objective and honest like no one else in your life can be. You play the same role for others as you bring your knowledge and experience to bear on the challenges facing other group members.

It's powerful to have someone (or multiple people) be able to "gut check" you when they think you're going down the wrong path, missing the critical issue at hand, or focusing on something that is not the real problem. In many cases, you're too close to the issue, and only an outsider has the perspective to the real issue or give you the push to stop avoiding it. They won't tell you something because they think it's what you want to hear.

You already realize that this sort of unfiltered advice from someone who doesn't have a financial stake in your success – but does want to see you succeed – is very hard to come by.

And these are all people you can trust, who are ready to help when no one else around you– not business partners, employees, friends, or family– can.

Access Knowledge That Only Comes With Experience

Your group members have got the scars, the well-worn experience to be able to speak credibly and authoritatively on the situation you are in and offer useful advice. They're all intelligent people, and have been successful in business.

Between the experience in their own businesses and the issues they've seen with dozens of other businesses through their broader network, they have a perspective that you can't buy anywhere.

Often, your Chief Executive Board *will* tell you what you want to hear. Confirmation from experienced CEOs you respect—when it's based on solid experience—can give you great confidence as you pursue a course of action. And, your peers often will be able to build on and improve your plan, based on their own business experience, potentially saving you months or years of learning curve.

As a business owner, you've had to make the tough decisions. Usually, all by yourself. Now you can bounce your ideas off others– colleagues and mentors. Left in a vacuum, you could be stuck making the same mistakes again and again. Because you're too close to the problem and emotionally invested in your business, you might miss a clear solution.

Having a group to stay accountable to – that also provides input and feedback – is a game-changer.

CHAPTER 8

Accountability

You already know that setting goals is one of critical ingredients of success in any endeavor in life. But, it's one thing to set goals and quite another to work towards achieving them.

When your goals are only known by yourself, it's all too easy to make excuses, hem and haw over the right direction to get to those goals, or even ignore them all together in favor of the easy route: business as usual.

But, you already understand that this is a recipe for stagnation and stalled growth. You understand that the fundamental changes your business needs won't happen unless you work towards your goals, making the tough decisions when necessary.

That's why accountability is a key feature of Chief Executive Boards. The impact of accountability on goal achievement is well documented.

According to a survey by the American Society of Training and Development, people are 65% more likely to achieve a goal after committing to another person to do so. The chances of success are 95% when there are ongoing meetings with accountability partner(s) to gauge progress.

Here's how it works with your CEO peer group:

1. You bring up a business, personal, or family-related issue you're struggling with at a meeting.

2. The group provides input and feedback on potential paths forward.

3. You are expected to make a decision and move forward, making some progress by the next time you meet. There is no excuse for not taking action and coming back to the next meeting with the same issue.

You're not obligated to follow the advice of the members of your board—you *can* change your mind about the path you want to take. The whole point is that you took action and learned something, even if it didn't pay off. But, no matter what decision you make, your peer group will make sure you follow through and hold you accountable.

By the same token, you must actively participate and offer the same to your fellow board members. They're not going to let slide that you were mired in inaction.

With the Chief Executive Boards, we've formalized this process.

During each forum meeting we have a process which members go through called "In Search of Balance." It's a way to add context to what's going on in somebody's life, their business, their goals… it's a status update of where they are.

As part of that process there is an accountability section where the group decides whether or not to hold them accountable for a certain goal… or whether they come clean with something they would like us to hold them accountable for.

During that conversation we, as facilitators, start by asking them about items on their "In Search of Balance" document. Have they made progress? If not, why?

It's typically under that sort of auspice and cadence that we hold members accountable. And sometimes some of the groups even have accountability partners that reach out to each other on a monthly basis to hold each other accountable.

CEBI facilitates accountability, as do the members, in a group setting and one-on-one. You can't escape. The idea is that you don't want to come to the next meeting without making progress.

The "In Search of Balance" document is a form completed by group members before each meeting containing information about:

- How you are tracking in your business, health, and life on a scale of 1 to 10
- Any positive or negative recent news about your business or personal situation
- Any pressing issues you have

In order to foster a healthy, safe environment for discussion, the facilitator leads by sharing their answers first. Then, other members follow, sharing items they want to discuss in-depth with the board.

Then, we get to the accountable items and personal and business goals. It's very visual, using a stoplight system. If it's red, that means you've made no progress. Yellow means you're making progress, but you haven't completed the task yet. If it's green, you've met or exceeded the goal.

In Search of Balance
5 Minute Update

Name:

Update on your business, personal and family developments including your issues / topics to be presented and discussed with the board members. Take into consideration major challenges and initiatives.

Topics	News – Positive and Negative	Pressing Issues		Life & Health Scores					
Business	Solid growth 1Q	Exploring growth pathways							
	New location in San Antonio, TX - 3Q	New verticals							
	Evaluate new marketing tools / approaches								
Personal	Sleeping better	Large Kidney Stone, surgery May 29th							
	Exercising regularly, lost 15 lbs	Selling primary home postponed							
	Home projects	A nightly bourbon							
		Tuned out TV News - depressing							
Family	G. started new job in Charlotte								
	Want time to focus on relationship with A.	Focus has been on business, properties, sons	Balance	Q1	Summit	Q2	Q3	Summit	Q4
			Life			8			
			Health			7			
Discussion Item How can we assist?	What capitalization strategies should I evaluate and consider for growing my business from $10M to $50M over the next 5 years?								
Accountable Items	Lose at least 6 lbs by 4Q - lost 15 lbs								
	Exercise at least 3 days/week. - joined gym, then started exercising at home when gym closed for COVID 19.								
				Q1	Summit	Q2	Q3	Summit	Q4
Personal Goals	Maintain weight a 165 lbs or less					3			
	Stay balanced throughout year - spiritually, physically, mentally					2			
	Help G. transition to new life in Charlotte					3			
				Q1	Summit	Q2	Q3	Summit	Q4
Business Goals	Extend business into 2 new geographies or verticals					2			
	Evaluate outside marketing firm for growing business					2			
	Maintain high retention and grow selectively					1			

CHAPTER 9

What Makes Chief Executive Boards Different

It's not your church, not the chamber, not your industry association...

You might be a member of your local chamber of commerce, participate in a networking group to get leads, or be in fraternal organizations.

A Chief Executive Boards forum meeting is not that.

It's a trusted group of like-minded business owners, CEOs, and presidents.

Each member:

- Is invited and vetted by the group itself.

- Must sign a mutual respect agreement which lays out the ground rules for effective participation and states that everything that is shared and discussed is confidential.

- Must feel comfortable being transparent and sharing their true vulnerabilities with the other members of the group.

Being part of a CEO peer group, gives you relationships with people at your level, who experience what you experience. They understand your stress, worry, relationship dynamics, and other issues. They know what you're going through because they've gone through the same thing.

A Chief Executive Boards forum is a network of peers like none other. Members can be vulnerable in the group; what is shared is completely confidential.

Valuable relationships extend beyond the peer forum. You have access to a broader network of CEBI members nationwide. As a member of CEBI, you may not have a direct relationship with them, but you are part of the same organization and can reach out– they will take the call.

We've formalized that process by hosting quarterly meetings and monthly check-ins, as well as National Summits, which brings in members from across the country to a central location.

We feature keynote speakers around the theme of the summit, which could be something like "When Life Meets Business." Members also present what we call executive briefings where they share experiences related to the theme.

Later in the day, the members break off into groups– a diverse group of individuals from different business around the country– distinct from their local board. This "national board" provides yet another forum to bounce ideas off of and broaden their network as they spend an intense two days together.

In recent times, we've stepped up the cadence of "virtual summits" in place of in-person meetings to continue engagement and plan to continue them in between quarterly meetings and national summits.

CEBI also hosts retreats at the board level at an exclusive location. An informal, pleasant setting – you're encouraged to bring your spouse– where abbreviated board meetings are interspersed with dinners, activities like playing golf, fishing, shooting sporting clays, adventures, and more.

It's all part of associating with successful people, developing deeper relationships among members, extending your support network, and give you access to more resources.

Does It Really Work?

Often, business owners can be skeptical walking into a situation like the board meetings and share closely held concerns with people they do not know, especially at the beginning. But soon enough, after they have seen others share, they open up, too.

It's like a ton of bricks has been lifted off their shoulders. We've even seen members cry, because they've been carrying such a heavy burden or are facing such a weighty decision... and they can finally have a group that understands and can offer meaningful advice in a safe and confidential setting.

Most importantly, we strive to be respectful. And, our cadence of meetings and events is not excessive and doesn't ask people to dedicate too much of their valuable time. We also understand that information overload could lead to overwhelm and prevent them from implementing what they've learned in the group.

By using a quarterly board meeting model, instead of a monthly meeting model, you ensure you don't get too many new ideas. Instead you get help with decision-making, execution, and accountability and have a time-line that makes achieving those goals possible. That's one reason our member retention rate is so high.

Importantly, we don't bring in subject matter experts like lawyers or CPAs, to speak to the group. Too often, they share a tidbit of information but are mostly there to pass out business cards and pick up new clients. We don't want our members to become a passive audience or be monetized in that way.

Boards are all about members helping members – no solicitation allowed. This is not networking for business development.

The purpose is to build relationships that support your growth as a business owner.

Peer Groups in Action

Recently, we were in a series of virtual meetings with CEO peer groups from two different parts of the country. As facilitators, we ask an open-ended question to jump-start the discussion on best practices:

"What changes are you making in your strategy or business in order to accommodate the new normal as it exists today?"

That gets people talking, sharing the moves or pivots they've made... or tools or strategies they're using.

By the end, you have 12 different ideas to get you thinking of how they could apply to your business– many approaches you probably had never considered before.

During local Chief Executive Board meetings, we will present content, usually in the form or concept or review of business concept or personal situation from a member, to stretch members' minds and encourage them to think in new ways.

Topics could be around leadership, business systems, how you're filtering information or delegating tasks, or anything else that could be applicable.

All this comes, not from outside experts, but from the trusted members of your CEO peer group. They share what they have implemented and what they have learned; you can ask questions and discuss how the approach could be applied to your business problems.

Of course, group members can bring up these sorts of issues, as well. Say you're thinking about changing up your marketing strategy. Somebody around the table will likely have some sort of experience— they can tell you what to avoid and what worked well.

Learning from their experience, helps you avoid missteps and reduce trial and error.

For example, Salesforce is the leading CRM system out there today. Most users are major corporations— but it's not necessarily the best CRM for small to midsize businesses.

A business owner thinking about implementing Salesforce could ask the group if anybody has experience with the system and get honest answers.

CHAPTER 10

How Chief Executive Boards Helped These Business Owners

What goes on at board meetings is, of course, confidential. But some members have agreed to share how their experience with CEBI has changed their business by offering fellowship, practical advice, support in tough times, accountability when working towards difficult goals, and more.

Scott Carr, President of Biotage, LLC

"Many, many times I came to a meeting with an issue and I was pretty certain on how to handle it... and they turned it upside down. And, I walked out with a completely different perspective, which was immensely valuable."

Scott joined Chief Executive Boards in 2012, seeking to bring some much-needed focus to his strategic planning. He credits his peer group with helping boost his revenue by more than 50% in just five years– and for an unexpected benefit in his personal life.

"Before I joined Chief Executive Boards, I thought my business was doing well. We were doing $24 million in revenue. I had what I thought was a good management team. But, we were focused on a thousand different things at one time. Looking back, I would say we were tiptoeing around key people and role issues.

"The most significant change in my business today after five years with CEBI, we've grown sales from $24 to $37 million. We've grown the operating income of the business from 6% to 16%. At the same time, we've reduced the operating costs to sales ratio by 20%. And on top of that, improved gross margins by 12% over the five years.

"A lot of that I would attribute to what I've learned, and the influence and input I've been given by CEBI members.

"CEBI has had an impact on my personal life that I didn't expect. I expected to go there and get business input, experience, having a board of advisors who would give me advice on my business. And what I found was a resource for my whole life, my personal life, as well as my business life. With equal interest in success period. Making Scott a success, not just Scott's business a success.

"The most significant benefits I've gotten from CEBI is it's a place you can go to talk about key business issues or key personal issues that you wouldn't share with your team, you wouldn't share with the next level executives if you're in a larger organization. Maybe you wouldn't even share at home.

"You get unbiased input from 100+ years of management and leadership experience in most boards, because of the time, tenure, and experience of the people around the table. You get input from functional talent that spans all aspects of operations and running a business. That is a key benefit that I get.

"You get very frank input. Your blind spots are revealed by these individuals giving you input. They expect the same from you. Many, many times I came to a meeting with an issue and I was pretty certain on how to handle it and I was simply looking for reassurance from colleagues and they turned it upside down and I walked out with a completely different perspective, which was immensely valuable."

Jennifer Guthrie, Owner / President of In Flight Crew Connections

"The board gave me some really solid advice and encouraged me to do what I needed to do. They held me accountable. They gave me a timeline of when I was supposed to contact them and tell them that I had done it."

After her business experienced a rapid rise in revenue, Jennifer discovered that the advice and accountability she got from her board helped her deal with internal issues, as well as growing pains during the transition from small to medium-sized business.

"I've been participating with Chief Executive Boards for four years. I had grown the business, and we had exponential growth. But my skillset wasn't necessarily to the same level and so the business had changed from a small business to a medium business.

"Now I have a sounding board of peers that I'm able to talk to and get advice from of what I need to be learning, doing, and working on. I get inspiration from others and things that they are going through.

"It gets lonely at the top. I had some internal issues that I knew I needed to deal with. But I didn't know what I should do. The board gave me some really solid advice and encouraged me to do what I needed to do. They held me accountable. They gave me a timeline of when I was supposed to contact them and tell them that I had done it.

"I have never left CEBI meetings, whether it's the local board or the National Summit, and felt like I wasted my time. It is a great group of peers. I love everything about it."

"My time is at a premium, as I am the CEO/Owner of a very fast paced and growing company... not to mention being a single mom of three active kids. Every local and national board leads me to walk away with such incredible insight and wisdom from my peers that open my mind to different perspectives and challenges me personally and professionally.

"The CEBI format helps me build quality professional peer relationships that hold me accountable! The time I dedicate to CEBI is never wasted. In fact, I schedule other priorities around CEBI."

Mike Thurow, President of

Spectrum Technologies

"We bring accountability to each other. Because in our business, who are we accountable to?"

Mike found it useful to be a member of an organization similar to Chief Executive Boards but says the time commitment was too extreme and the opportunity to talk out business issues with fellow members too limited.

"I've been a member of Chief Executive Boards for at least eight years. I've been a founder of Spectrum for 30 years. But before joining Chief Executive Boards, I was a member of good organization called Vistage that brought a lot of value but was very time-consuming. It was at least one day per month to attend a Vistage event that had some value but took me away from the business of running Spectrum.

"You only had an opportunity, once a year, when you hosted an event, to present maybe a business plan and get feedback. That just wasn't good enough.

"The real value of CEBI that I wasn't getting at Vistage is that every time there is a local board meeting you get the opportunity to process an issue, to have 30,

45 minutes to get feedback, and act on the feedback they give you. That's priceless.

"Accountability is the key word. We bring accountability to each other. Because in our business, who are we accountable to?"

Brad Loetz, President of Remedi

"You always get that one idea that pays for your time and attendance."

As a new business owner, Brad found Chief Executive Boards to be instrumental in making steady progress towards his goals.

"I've been participating in Chief Executive Boards since 1999. The status of my business and life prior to joining was that of a novice and early business owner. Since I've been a member of Chief Executive Boards, my life and business has obviously improved to continue to be involved for so many years.

"I leverage Chief Executive Boards as a board of advisors. I have access to inquire and get assistance for just about any problem that I have. I've been helped with not a lot of home runs, but a lot of singles and doubles at local and national boards.

"You always get that one idea that pays for your time and attendance. So the people who tend to gravitate towards and get the most value out of Chief Executive Boards are those folks who are doing well but know there is room on the runway for getting better."

CHAPTER 11

Conclusion

By this point, you should be ready to make a major change in the way you do business.

You want to create a business you can work *on*, not *in*. You want to delegate tasks you don't like or aren't effective at to those on your team who are more capable. You want to work less and enjoy life more.

While at the same time you want to grow your business into a cash engine that provides personal wealth now and sets you up for a well-deserved payday down the road when you sell.

To turn your business into a cash engine now, one that has potential for a big cash event when you sell at retirement, you need to plug into Chief Executive Boards.

When you don't have access to your business peers, a group of likeminded folks who provide an impartial sounding board, who hold you accountable as you work on your business's most pressing problems, help you spot the solutions – and even opportunities – that are in your blind spot, and provide support and guidance on any business – or even personal – issue you're dealing with... you'll continue to suffer and struggle.

Like you, the members of your peer group won't always have it together completely. But, you're all committed to helping each other get it all together.

When you surround yourself with group of peers who are going where you're going, you have the ideal group to help and support you. They make the journey to building your business into a venture sustainable in the long term much easier.

If you choose not to go that route, you're stuck. Your future will look like your present, and it'll be hard to break the pattern.

There are local Chief Executive Boards located throughout the United States. At each quarterly meeting you can expect:

1. At least one new idea or takeaway

2. Accountability for your actions
3. Confidential sources to reach out to when you have issues, needs, or challenges
4. The chance to bond with your peers
5. Guidance when you are off track, or confirmation when you are on the right track
6. The ability to contribute to the success of others

Chief Executive Board International's role is to facilitate meetings and provide other resources. As a CEBI member you also get:

1. **Peer Advisement** – This provides real life experiences from leaders who have experienced similar situations. Developing a relationship with a local board gives our members a support group they can depend on and reach out to in times of crisis (business or personal).

2. **National Summits** – A strong gathering of peers from across the country – not only for networking, but as an additional group that can provide insight and feedback on any pressing issues.

The National Summits schedule speakers on current situations / trends as well as on general topics that members have specifically requested they want to learn more about.

3. **Executive Retreats** – This provides couples with time to themselves, with additional opportunities to engage with other couples at these 2 or 3-day retreats. Everything is coordinated, allowing for a stress-free vacation with time for couples to focus on each other and their marriage.

   This also provides time for spouses to share struggles they may have with being married to the owner (or CEO) of the company, and the obstacles that go along with that. It can provide an atmosphere for spouses that lets them know they are not alone in having to compete with the business for time.

4. **Workshops** – These are developed based on needs shared from the members. The workshops are ultimately for members as well as their key staff members and focus on a primary topic. The sessions are typically for two days – and are limited in number to provide for more intense training.

5. **CEBI Website Resources** – There are a multitude of resources on our website, including presentations on various topics, made at our National Summits. These are available 24 hours a day and a member can browse through to find subjects of interest.

   There are also a significant number of business forms as well as outlines – that can help a member dial in to an issue. Previous webinars are also available on our website, as is registration for upcoming ones.

Chief Executive Boards is a selective group, and each prospective member must meet certain criteria before being offered to be a part of the CEBI membership:

- A desire to always be growing and learning.
- A willingness to seek out alternate information and opinions.
- No hesitation in asking for help and direction.
- An open mind is listening to suggestions brought forward by the peer group.
- An interest in seeking out others who can help them make their business better.
- A lack of ego – you can't be someone who thinks they already know everything.

- A readiness to take action, regardless of whether they're taking advice from the group or not.
- An attitude that embraces accountability.

Whenever you're ready here are three ways we can help increase your profits:

1. Subscribe to the Lessons From The Boardroom podcast to hear from CEOs and owners of small to medium-sized businesses, experts, and thought leaders who will help you find greater clarity and create more freedom in your business.

2. Hear real-world stories from CEOs like you, who are using the principles of this book to build more successful businesses, make more money, and create balanced lives. Go to:

   ChiefExecutiveBoards.com/testimonials

3. Learn if participation in Chief Executive Boards International is a fit by calling 864-527-5917, visiting ChiefExecutiveBoards.com or send an email to info@chiefexecutiveboards.com

An original native of Greenville, South Carolina, Kevin graduated university from The Citadel, located on the beautiful coastal banks of Charleston, South Carolina. After receiving his business degree Kevin began his career with the Fluor Corporation, one of the world's largest engineering and construction companies.

Throughout his 20+ year career with Fluor he excelled through the ranks to became Vice President of sales and operations in the U.S. and multiple countries where he navigated existing and start-up operations through challenges, downturns, scale-ups and success.

Kevin was later recruited by Rental Service Corporation as Vice President of Sales and Operations where he helped lead the company out of a recession plagued environment to an ultimate sale to United Rentals Corporation for an unprecedented industry multiple.

Following his heart, Kevin's next career adventure led him toward helping private business owners and leaders to succeed not only in business, but also with an enhanced quality of life. An ensuing purchase of Chief Executive Boards International facilitated this calling in which Kevin re-energized a legacy organization to provide an elite, business leader peer advisory growth and development experience.

After multiple assignments throughout the world, Kevin continues to lead Chief Executive Boards International and enjoys facilitating the platform with which company leaders throughout the U.S. improve their business and life fulfillment. When he's not working to assist others with their success, he enjoys personal adventures and living in South Carolina with his wife, Angelina.